Cuba

A Poetography Travel Journal

by Doug D'Elia

Cuba

ISBN-13: 978-1-365-14314-4

www.dougdelia.com
Email: dougvandelia@gmail.com
⬛ : Doug Delia

Printed in U.S.A

Introduction

I didn't expect to hear a Cuban band playing Bob Dylan, but then again, I saw and heard many things in Cuba I didn't expect. I didn't expect to hear a barbershop quartet singing four part harmonies, or a twelve-piece cappella choral group performing Americana folk songs and Africa chants.

I didn't expect to see a state sponsored dance company performing on the second floor in a downtown Havana studio. I didn't expect to hear a sixty-piece orchestra of young talented musicians performing Bolero while young men performed on scaffolding and girders. I didn't expect to hear a jazz band whose members had performed at jazz clubs in New Orleans, and the Lincoln Center in New York City.

I didn't expect to see local fashion models from the Chanel Runway Show practicing in the lobby of the National Hotel. I didn't expect to see the three-story Fabrica de arte Cubano, Havana's equivalent of MOMA, where the art of emerging artists mixes with instillation and performance, where patrons sip Cuban coffee at the cafes or rum at the bar. I didn't expect to see film crews filming along the Medicon or at Hemingway's Finca Vigia. I didn't expect to see hundreds of Cubans crowding onto the pier to greet the American passengers aboard the first Cruise ship in 50 years to anchor in the waters of Havana Bay.

But the biggest surprise was the Cuban people and the great love and respect they have for their culture and artistic roots. Yes, there is economic poverty, the country is still reeling from a half century of economic sanctions, but the Cuban peoples have been the beneficiaries of years of free high quality education and state sponsored support of the arts, and they are eager and ready for collaborations and partnerships where they can share their talents and enthusiasm for the arts.

Like other Americans, I wanted to get to Cuba before it "changed," but it had already changed. The Cuban people have initiated a new revolution, and they are poised to become not only the cultural and artistic epicenter of the Caribbean, but the entire world. Go there not to see the change, but to be a part of it.

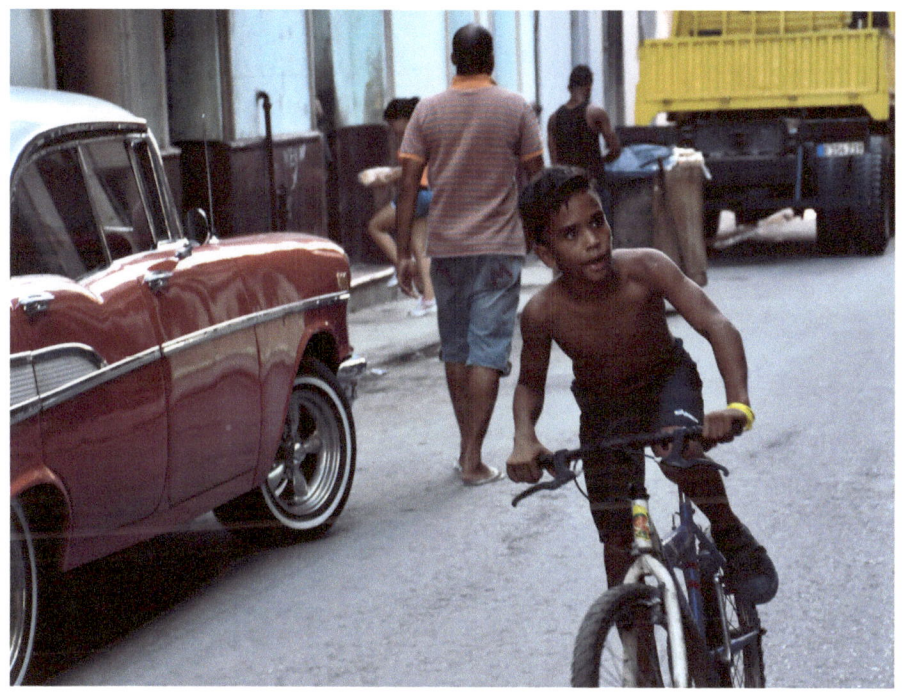

All mothers see their sons in this boy,
men see themselves.

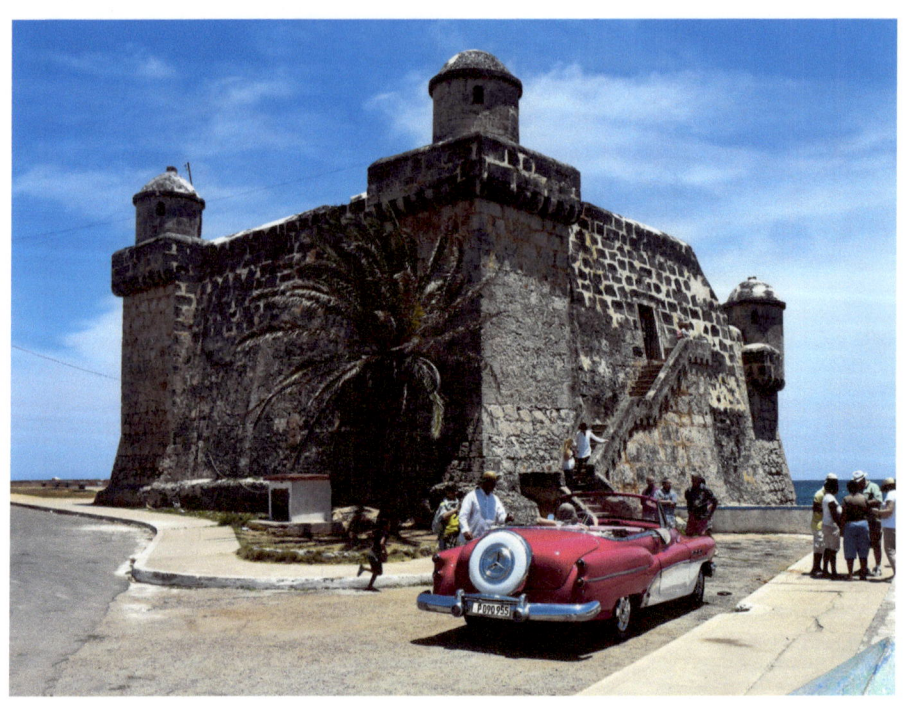

There is a fort built over Caribbean waters
where souvenirs and memories are traded freely,
upwind of gun and rumrunners.

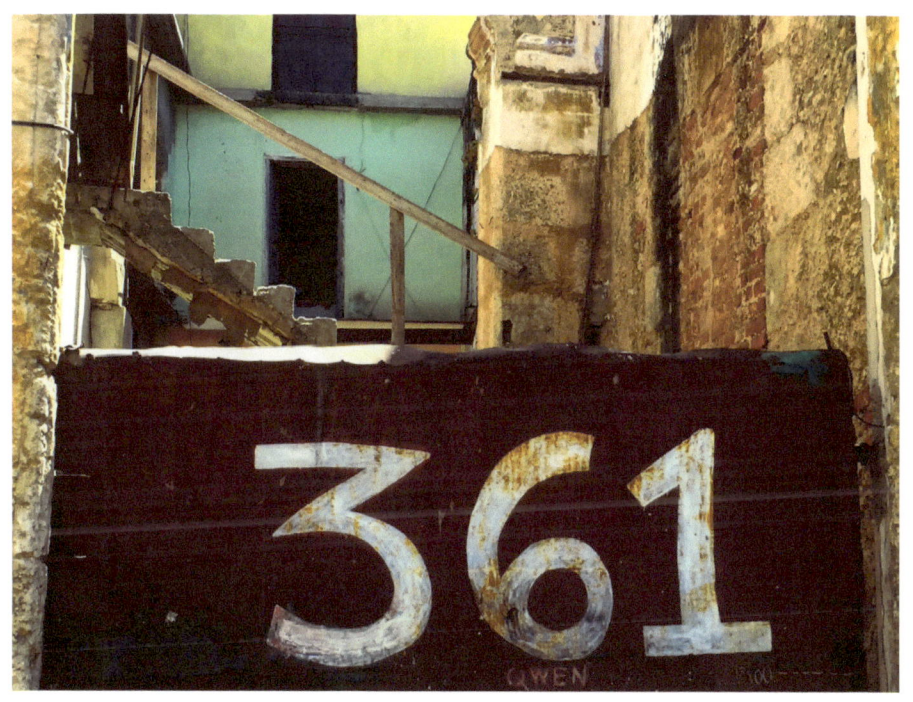

When the names of those who
lived
in this place have faded from
memory,
the numbers that remain will
serve as beacons.

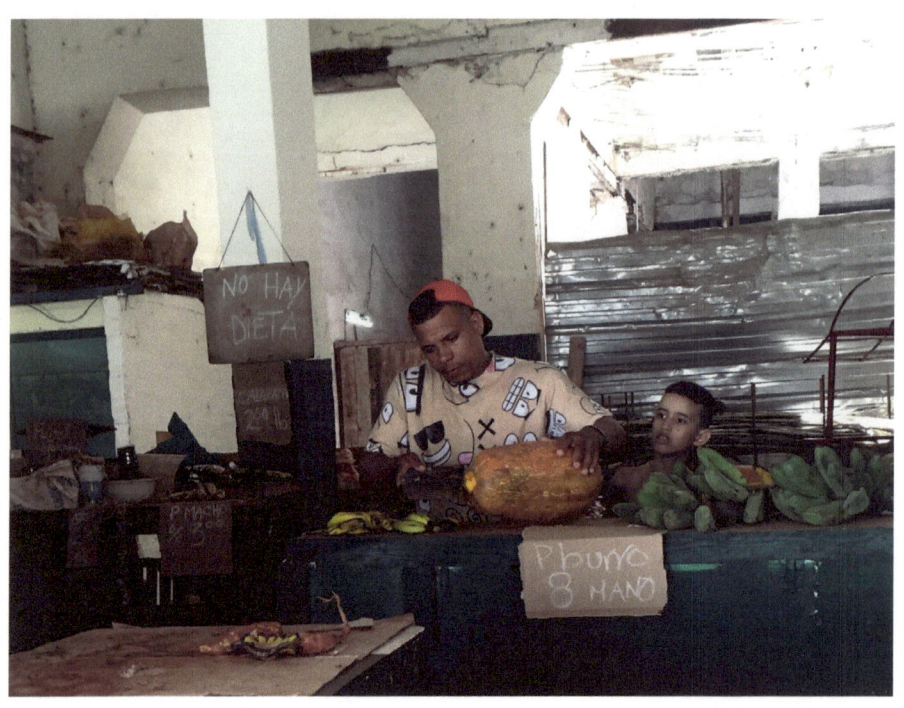

The real fruits of our labor
can be found in the eyes of our children.

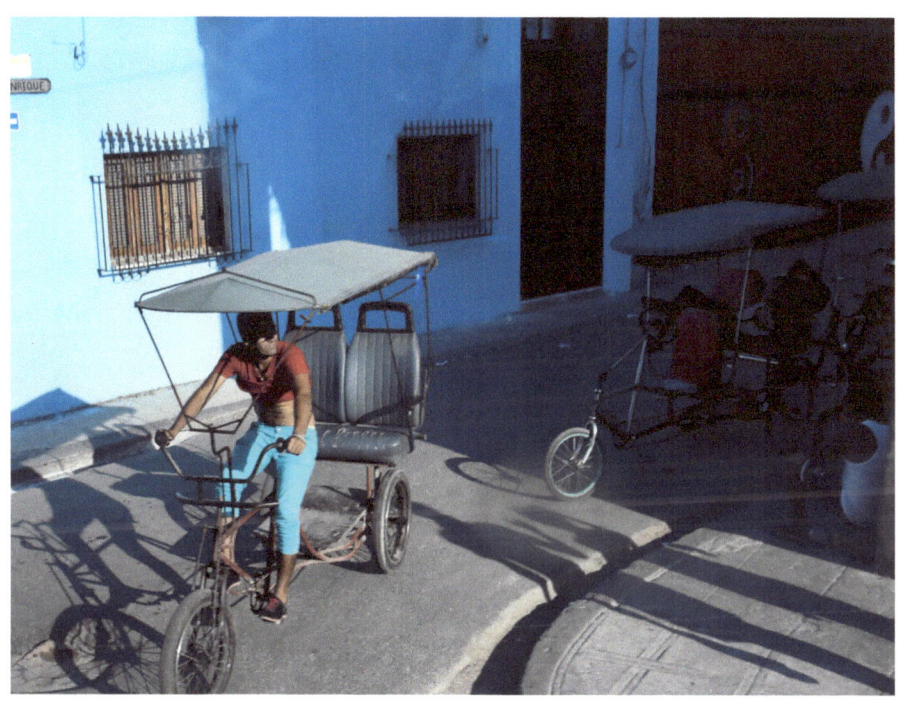

A bicycle taxi driver slows to pick up
the shadows of two tourists
standing at the corner.

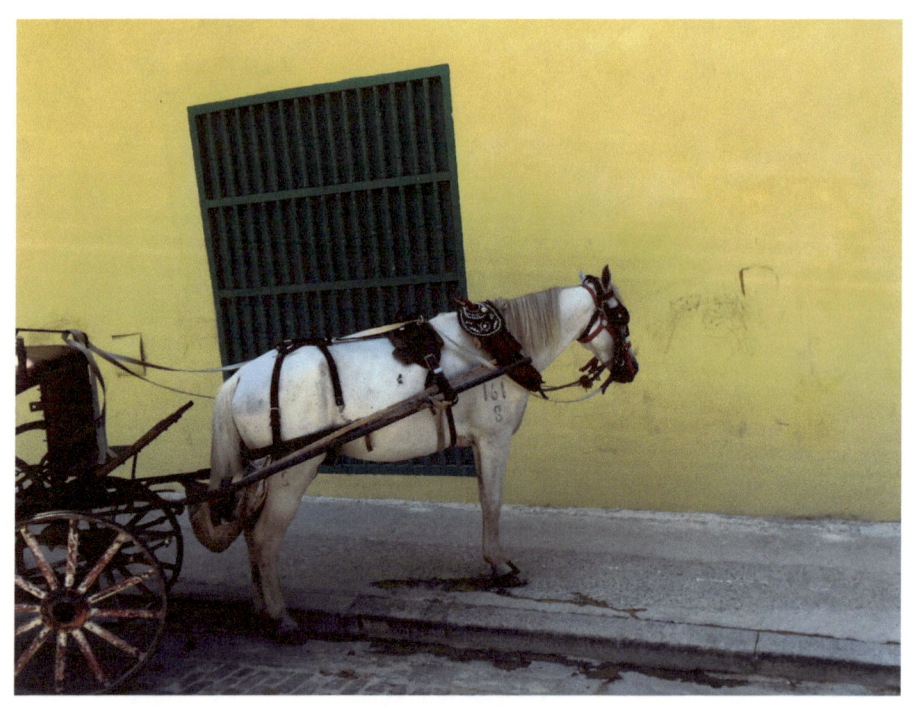

I love the hue
of Havana Yellow
two hoofs above
street level.

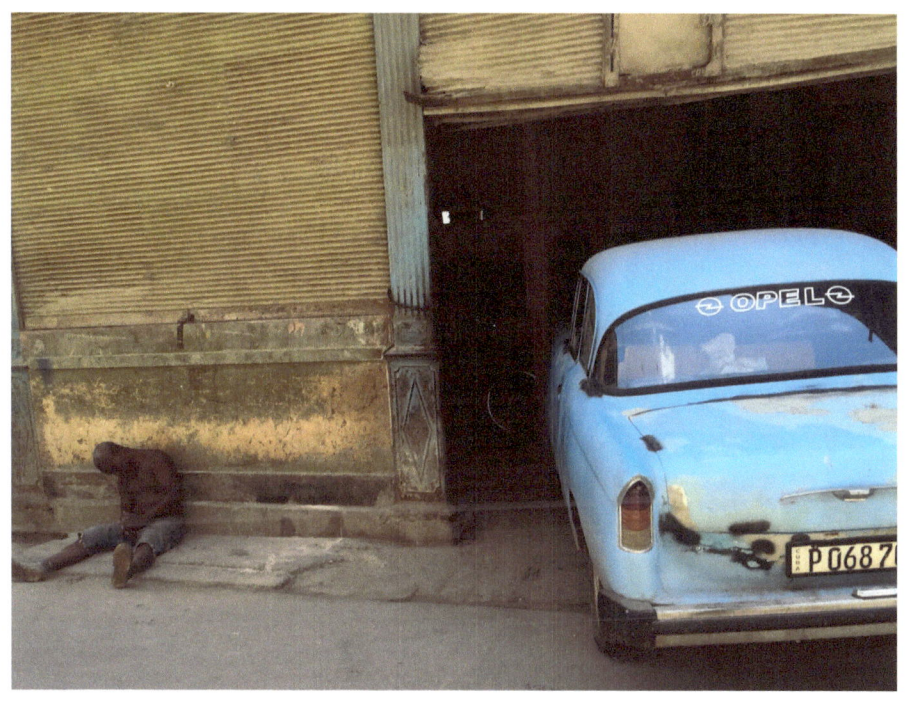

Slouching towards Havana.

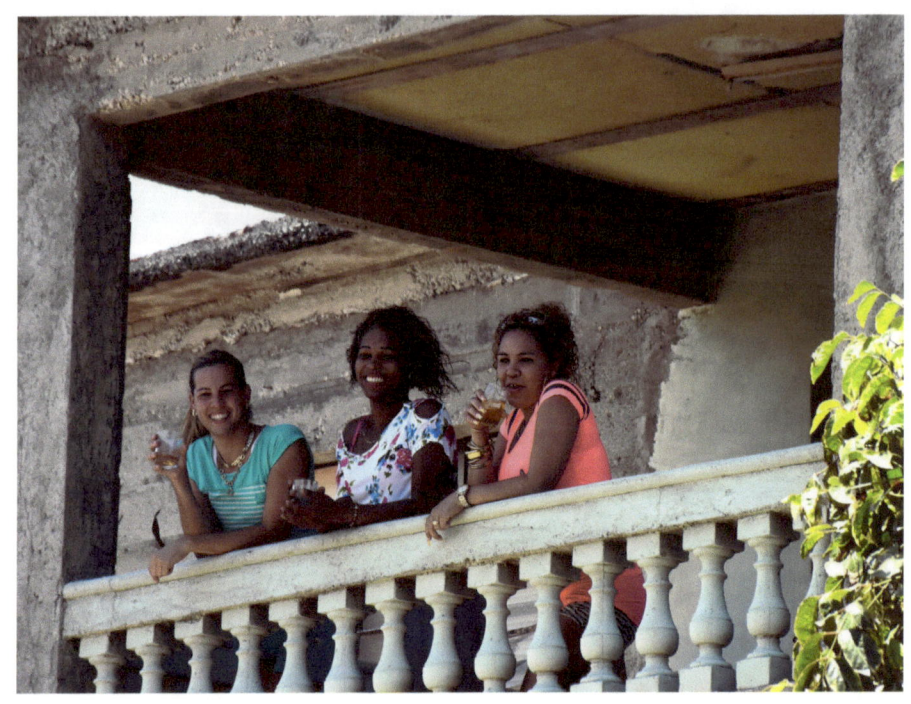

Senoritas waving
like human flags
made of rum and smiles.

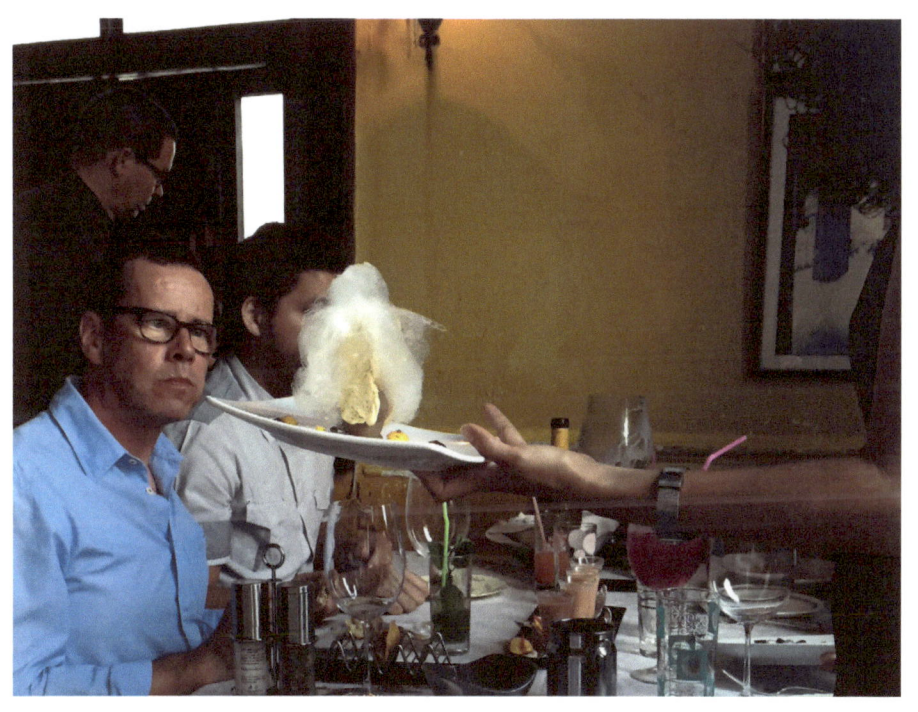

Dessert in drag.

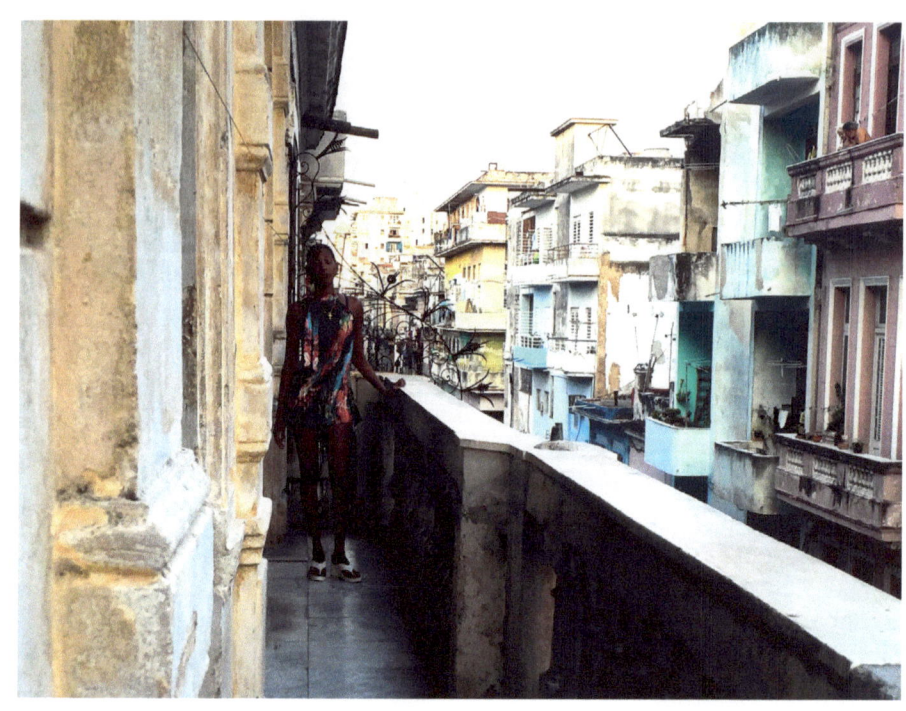

When you want to restore beauty
to an old building, it is best
to begin with the balcony.

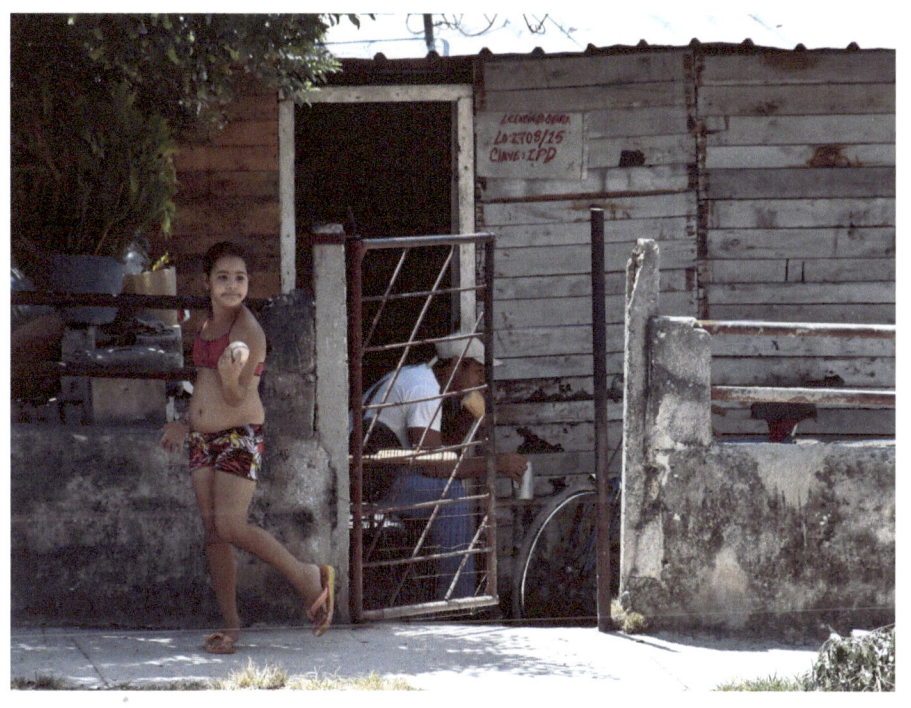

A reliever in summer uniform
practices her curveball in the bullpen,
while the pitching coach relaxes on
a nearby bench.

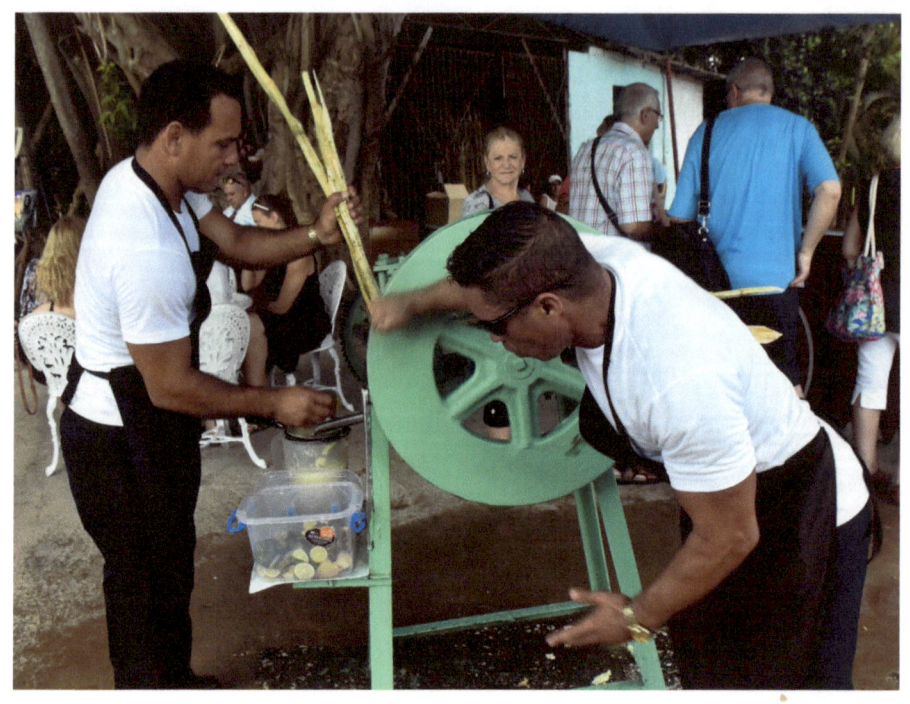

Bring the cane that we
might beat it into pulp,
and drink to the destruction
of all weapons.

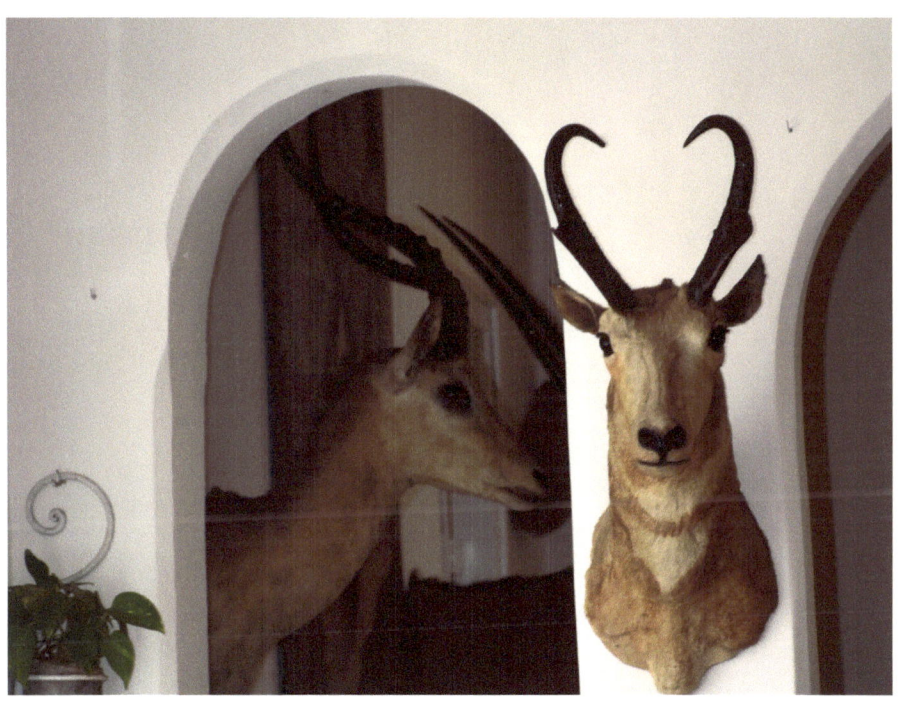

Hemingway's villa,
where he writes under
the dead-eyed gaze
of fur and horn.

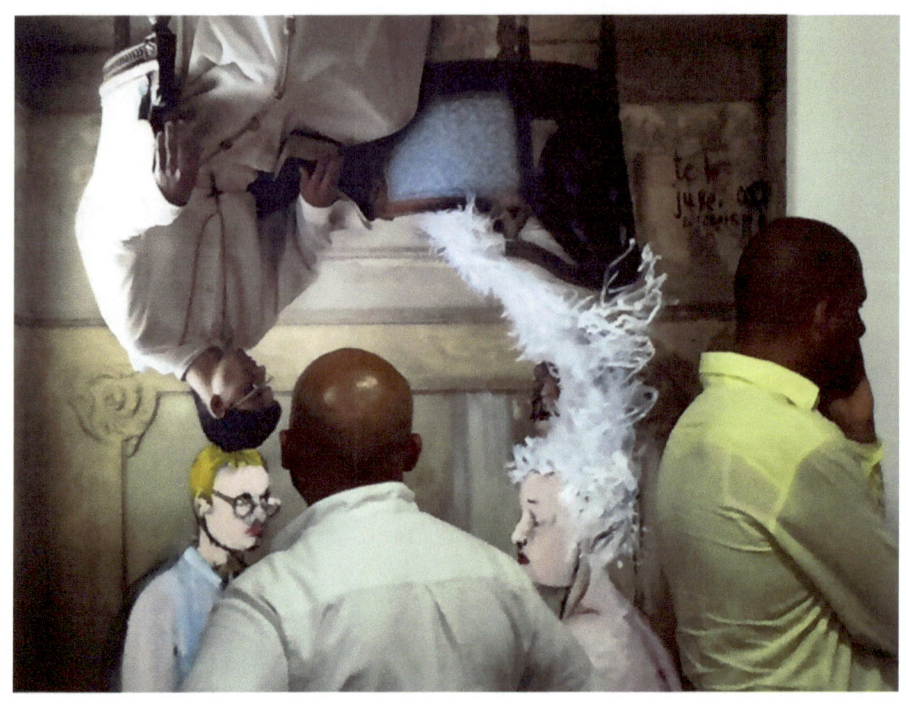

The young Pope,
hears the confession of an Artist
in front of, and upside down to,
the ease dropping crowd.

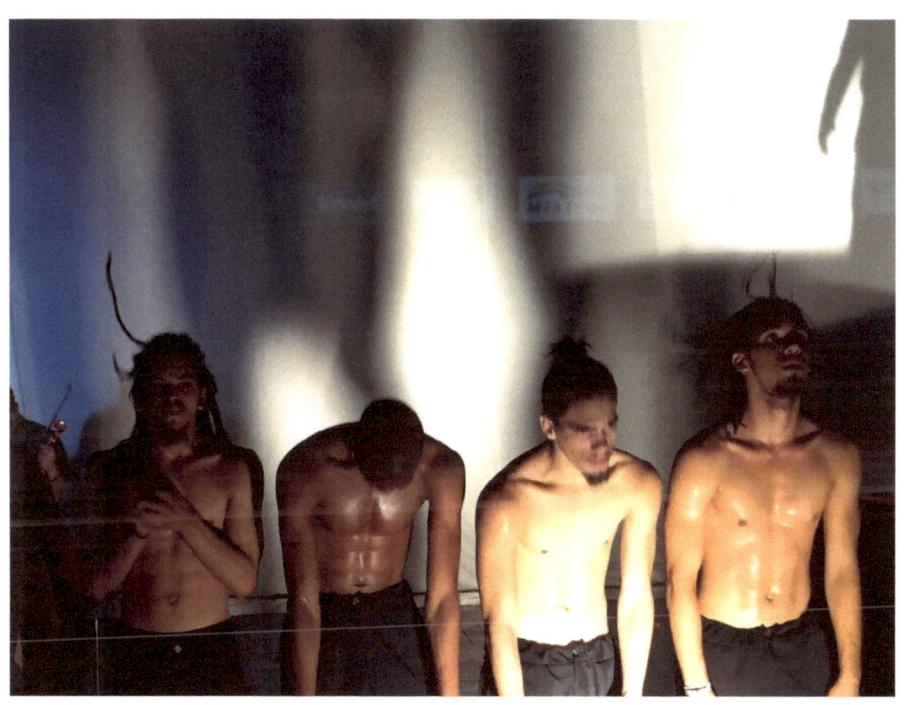

There is a light within,
a certain kind of light,
that can never be fully contained.

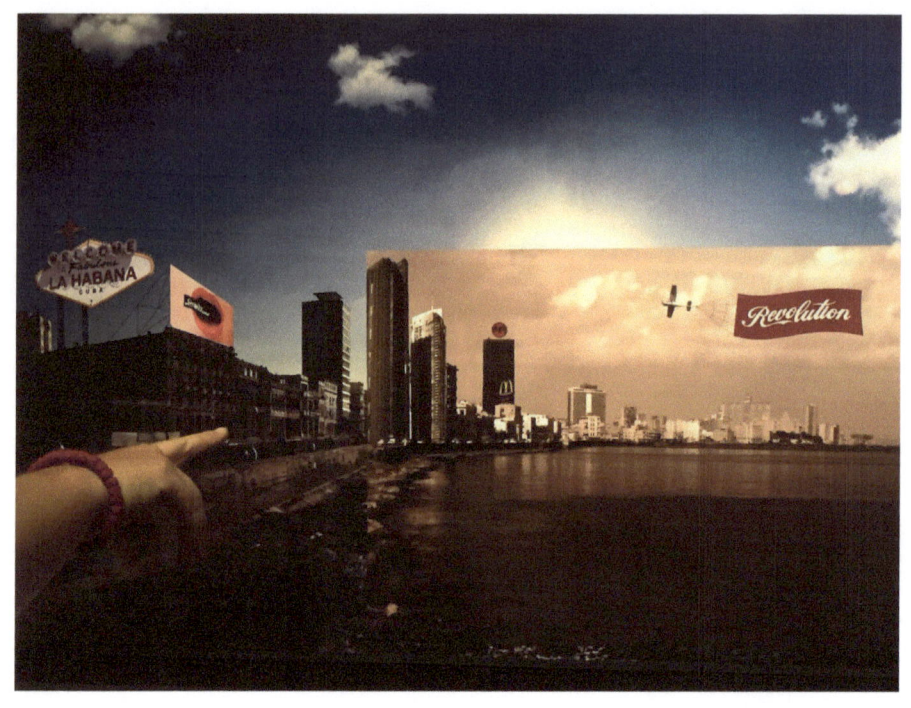

After the first McDonald's
appeared along "The Malecon,"
the revolution began in earnest.

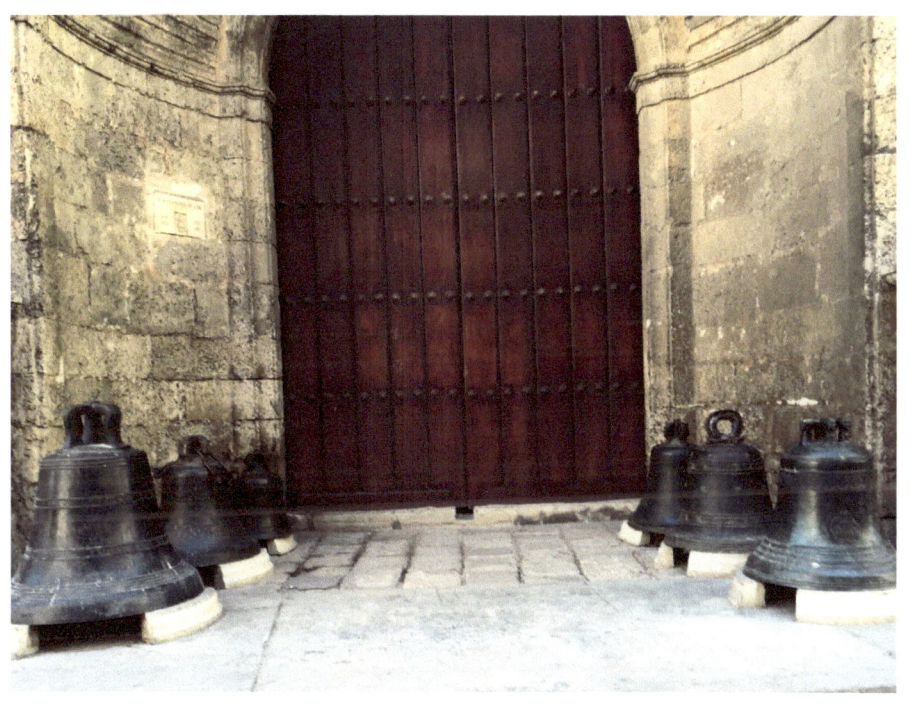

The building once a church is now a school,
but the spirit of love and communion
lives on in the hearts of those
who once rang the bells.

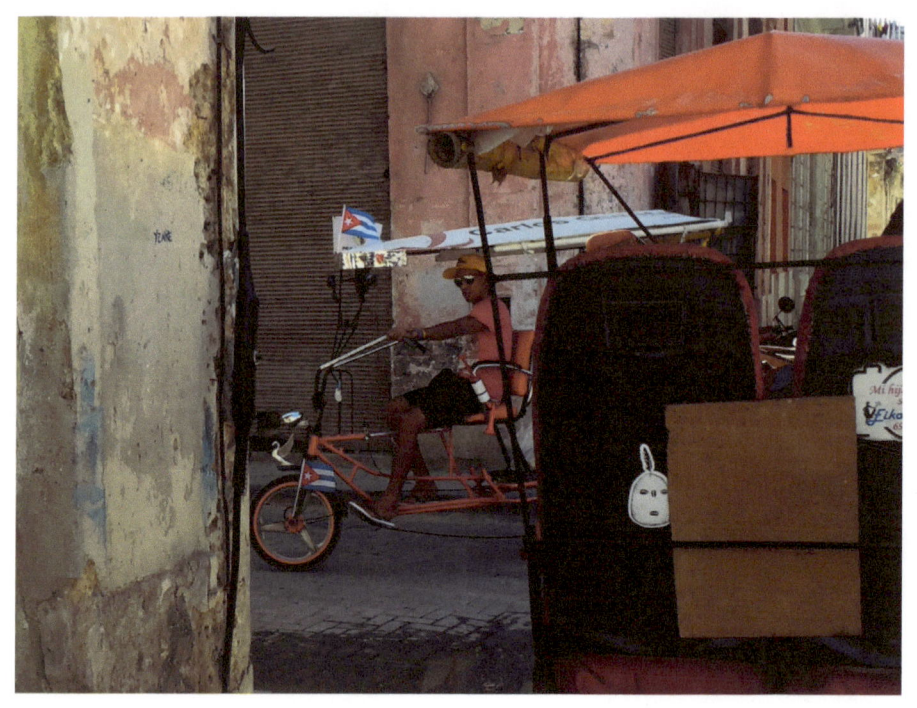

A fleet of foot soldiers
criss crossing Havana
in search of pesos.

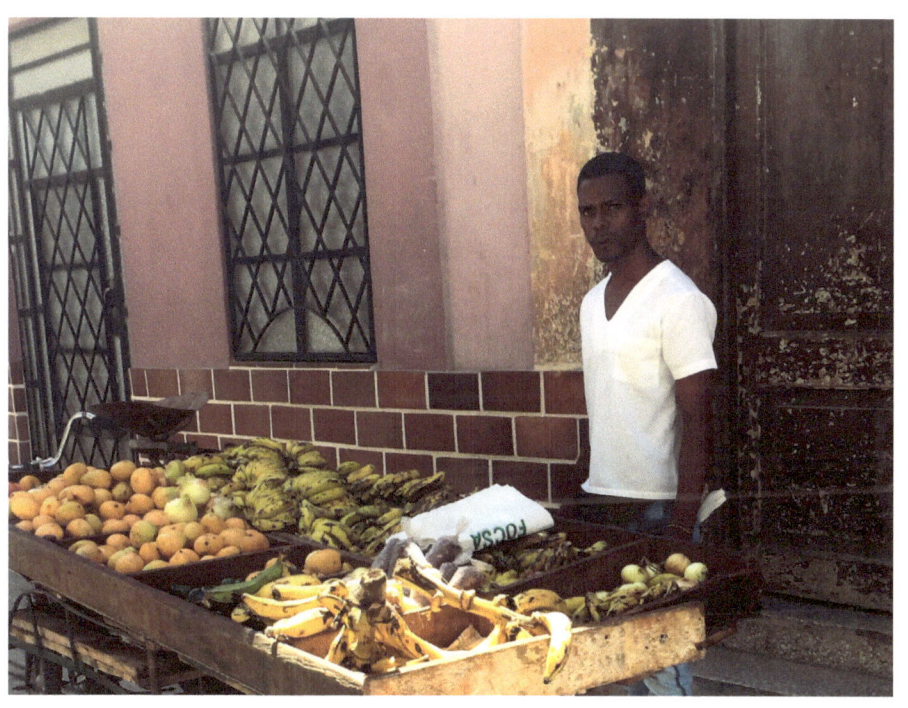

Come Mister Tallyman…

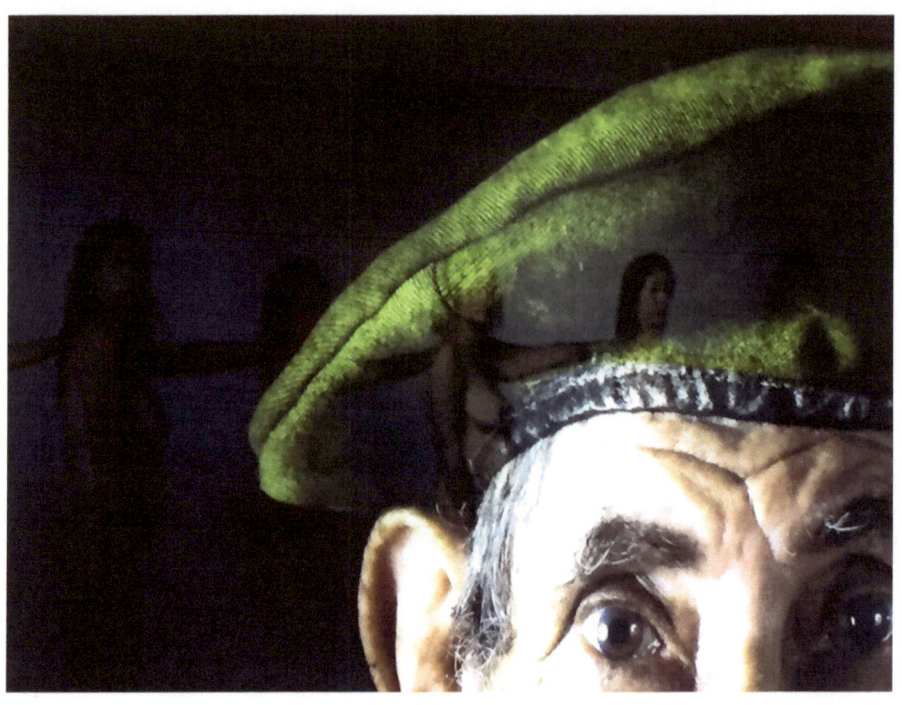

In my dream a line of sugar plum fairies danced the rumba in my head.

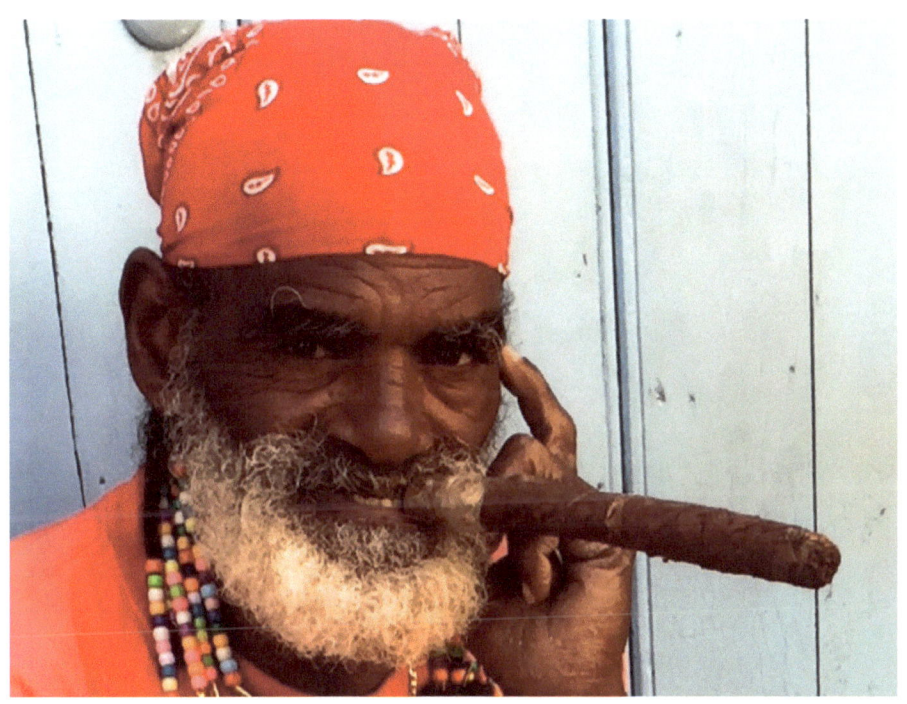

He wraps his cigar with tape,
hoping it will withstand
one more season of tourists.

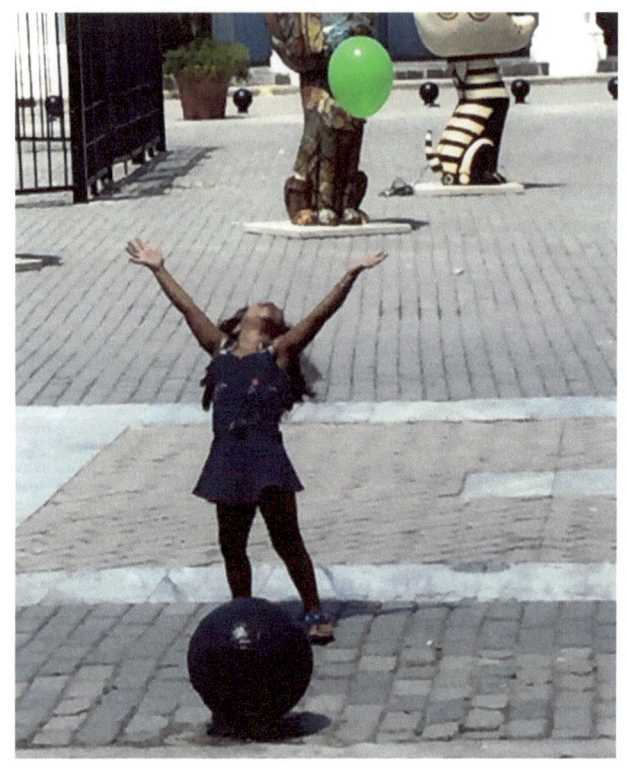

Turning cannon balls into balloons.

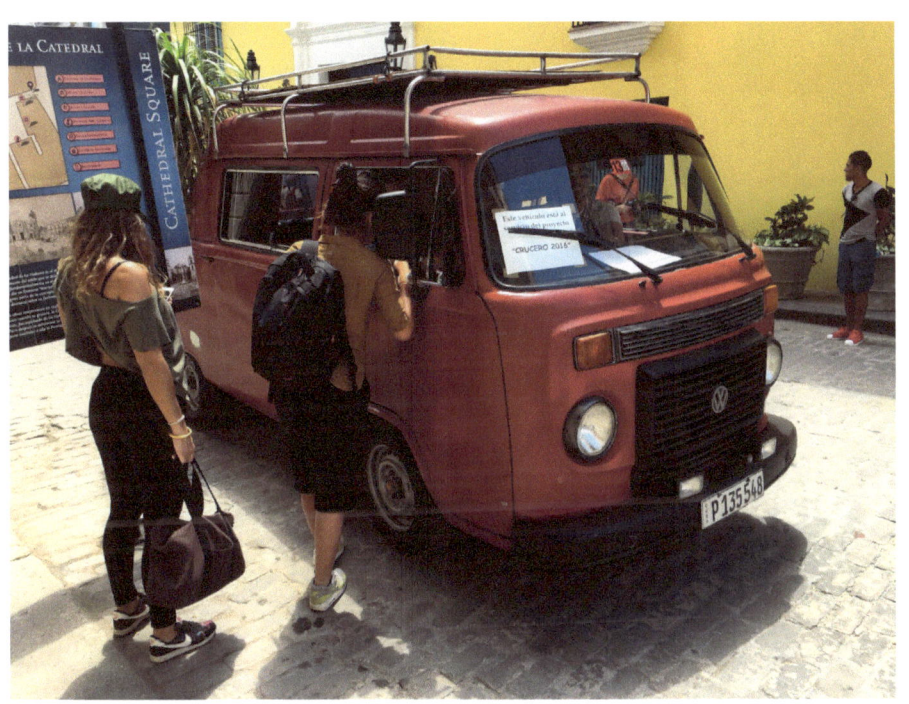

I can take you as far as San Francisco.

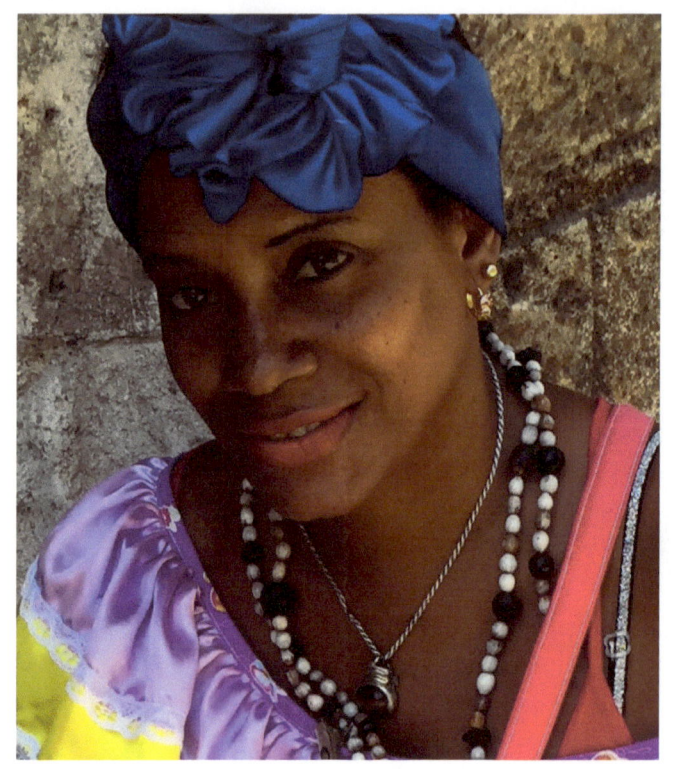

The costumbrista,
characters of romantic novels
and poetic verse roaming the plaza
one league ahead of the Conquistadores.

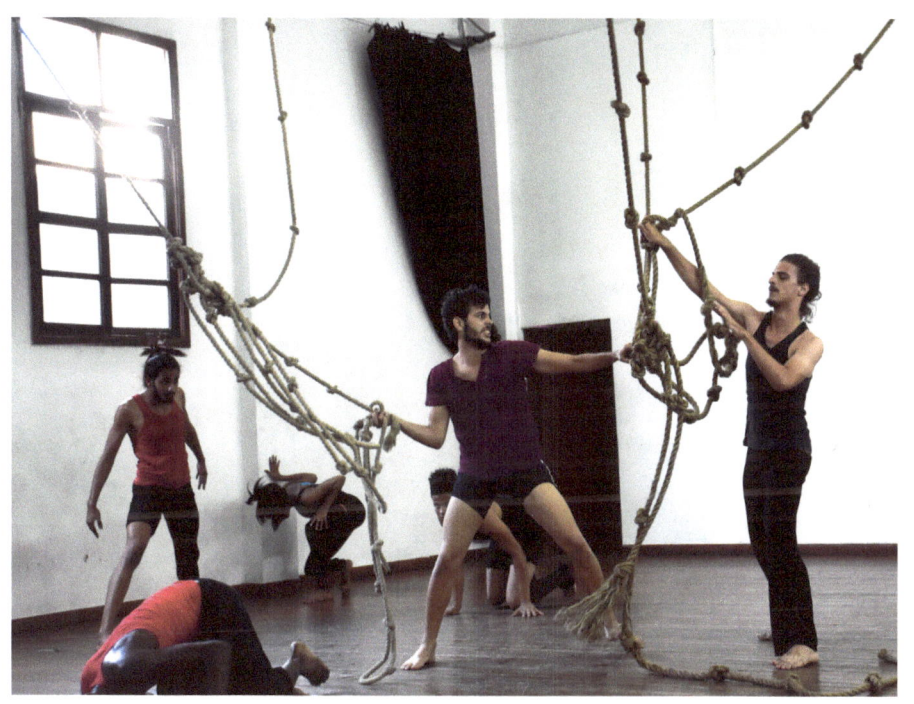

A nation that doesn't support
the art of its people
will never free itself from
the wheel of war.

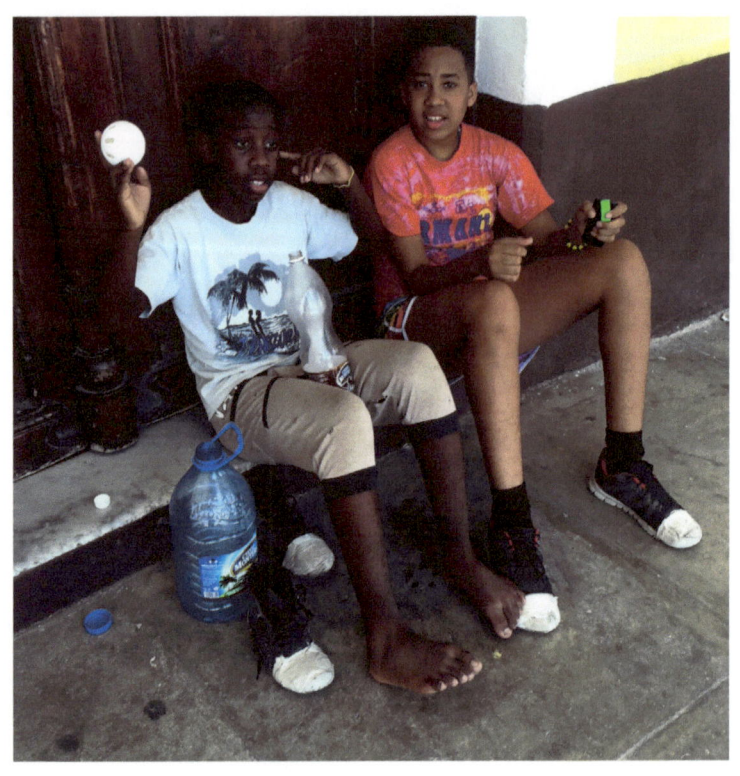

I think a future in baseball
is possible, if I can keep my shoes
from falling apart.

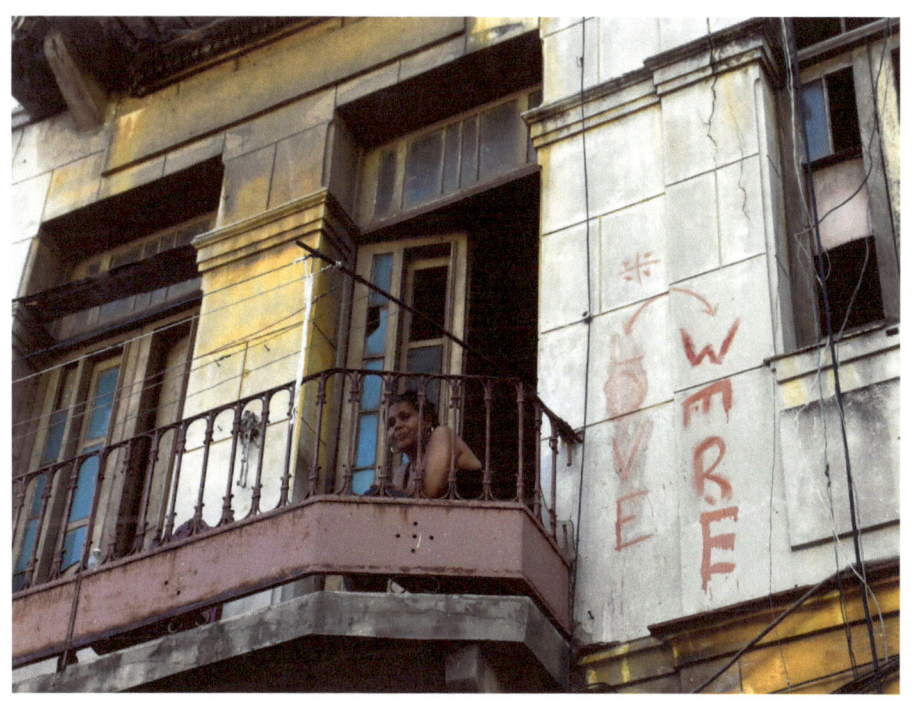

At times it is difficult to make sense of Love.

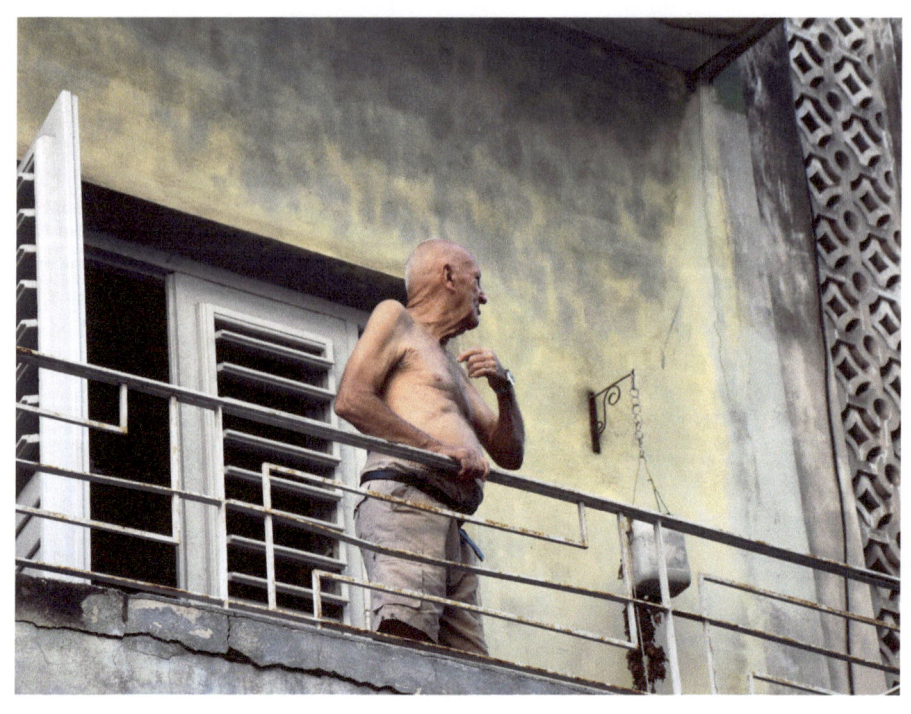

Morning becomes Electra
minus the New York Times.

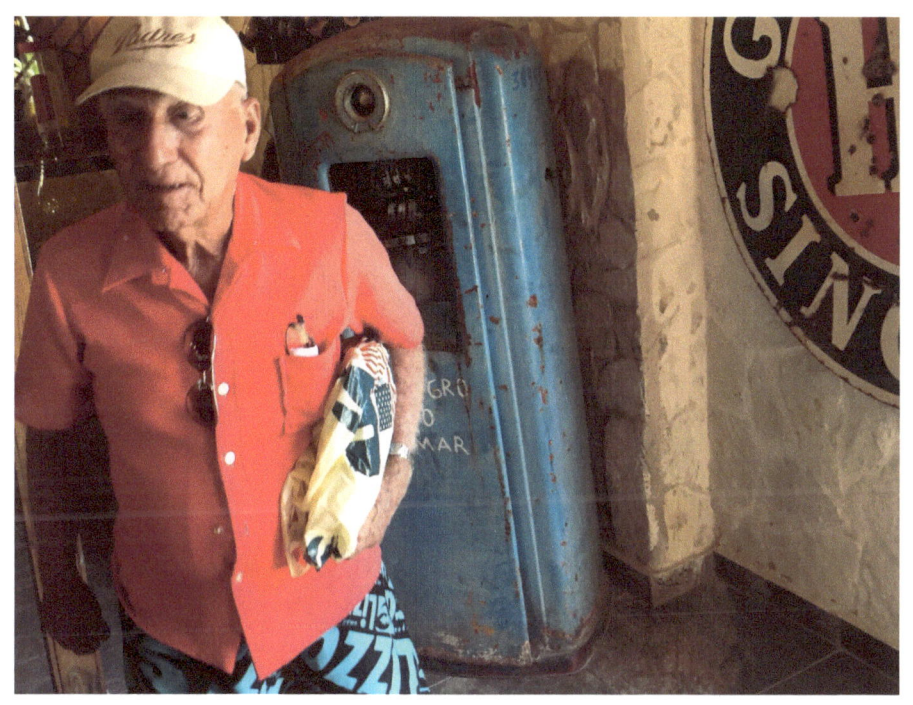

Captain, Oh Captain!
fishing these waters since he was a boy,
since Papa Hemingway smelling of Marlin
sent him to buy rum.

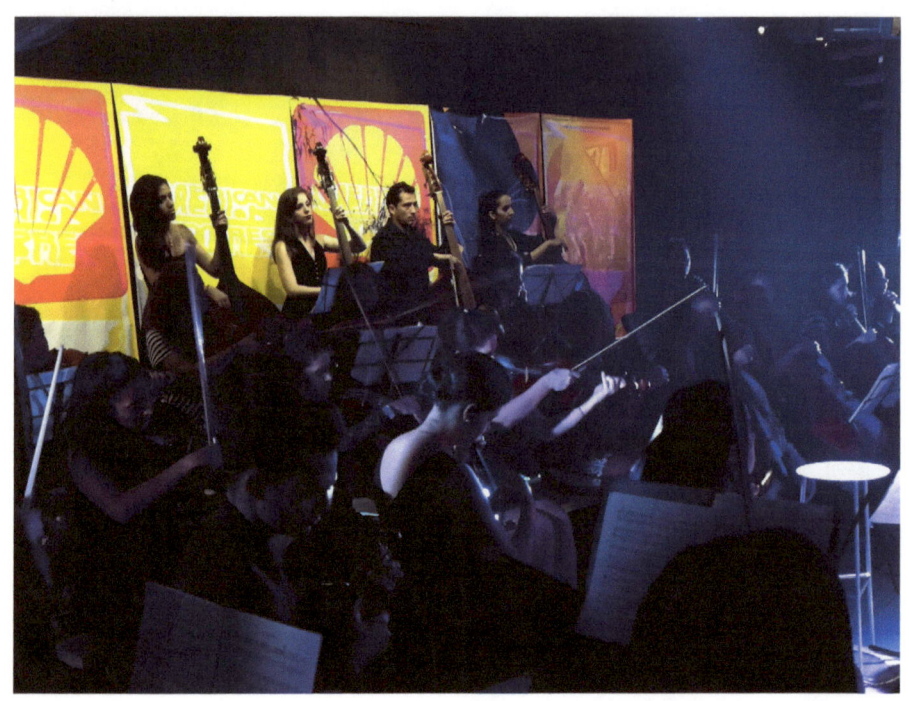

The next revolution will televised,
as we stand in awe of an orchestra
that plays us symphonies on instruments
repurposed from weapons,
and tuned to peace.

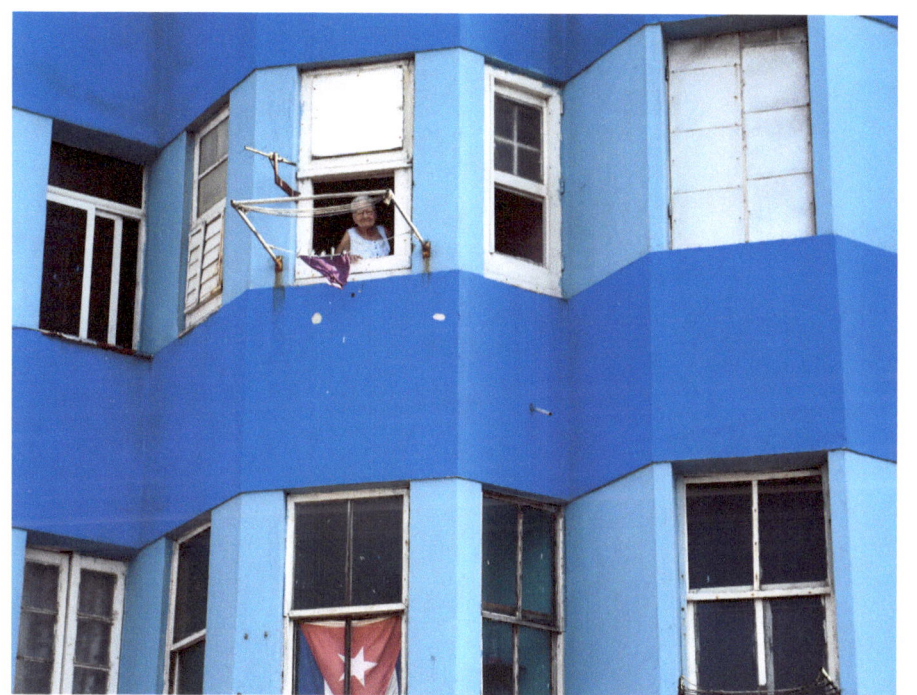

A nation has become truly liberated when
its citizens fly their flag and underwear
from the same windows.

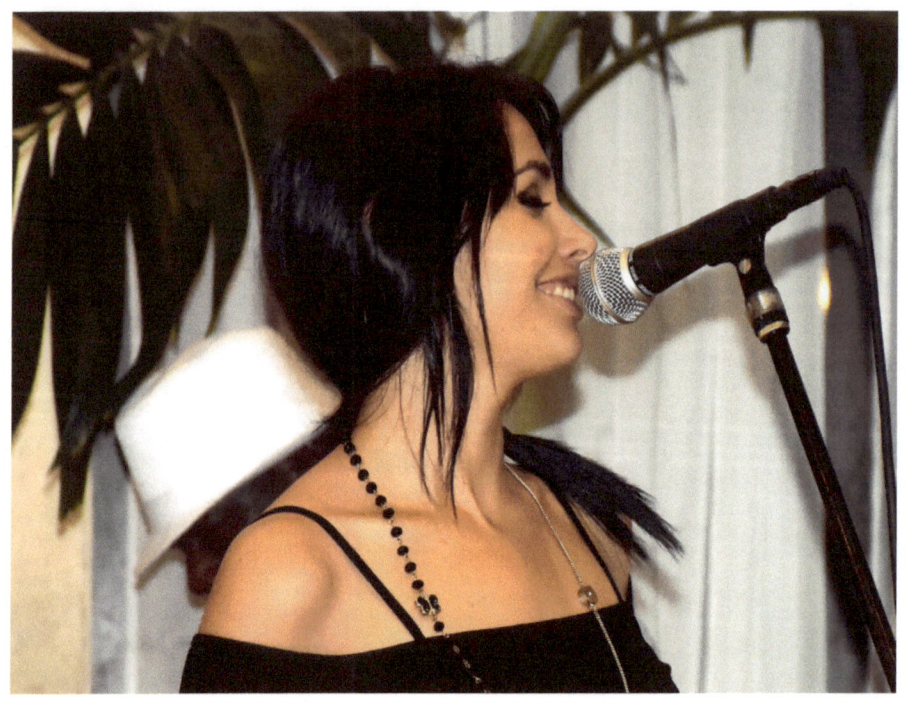

When we were slaves our cries were songs
sung in minor keys, but now our howls have turned
into poems, melodic cantos depicting the struggle
of a nation that measures its voices
as gross national product.

Boho Recommendation

When the cab driver pulled up in front of the restaurant La Guarida, I thought that I had given him the wrong address. Certainly this couldn't be the entrance to one of Cuban's top rated restaurants? The entry way opened into a courtyard that was obstructed by a bright red "Men at Work" sign, leaving the wide dusty marble staircase with wrought iron railing and hand carved banister, as the only way to the second floor. The ascending wall was decorated with a mural of Ché and a quote from Fidel.

The stairway led to an open floor plan second floor, with portals that opened to a beautiful balcony that overlooked the street. An Italian photographer was photographing a Cuban model on the balcony with colorful Havana as a backdrop. The staircase continued on to the third floor, and the restaurant's hostess station. A word of caution here – you need a reservation – and the restaurant's online automated response (in Spanish) is not a reservation. La Guarida is special, featuring beautiful title floors and polished wood décor, with some tables overlooking the street, a diverse menu and exquisite food. The creative bathroom is unisex, and the room at the end of the hall, which could easily pass as the women's powder room is a private residence, but they seemed quite used to customers entering their living room and were very welcoming to those who mistook it as part of the restaurant. The restaurant is privately operated, and was featured in the 1993 film, Fresca and Chocolate.

The cab driver returned at nine o'clock, right on schedule, and the next stop was Fabrica de Arte Cubano, an old church converted into an art space. Fabrica de Arte Cubano is a gallery featuring painting, sculpture, installation art, film, dance, photography, music, theatre, and performance art. There is also a café, and both a ground floor and rooftop bar. I saw a fifteen-minute dance/theatre performance with a live sixty-piece orchestra. I recommend getting there before 10pm, that's when the locals arrive and the line wraps around the corner. Oh, there is an admission – it's two pesos – the equivalent of two U.S. dollars.

www.ingramcontent.com/pod-product-compliance
Lightning Source LLC
Chambersburg PA
CBHW041133200526
45172CB00018B/268

*9 7 8 1 3 6 5 1 4 3 1 4 4 *